THANKS
GOD

YOU'RE A REAL PAL

JOE CURTIS

Published by:
First Return Press,
23 Upper Mount Street,
Dublin 2, Ireland

First Edition: 1998
Reprinted: 2009

ISBN: 978-0-9533320-2-1

© **Copyright**: Joe Curtis

CHAPTER 1

Hello! My name is Susan. I have been friendly with God since I was about 30-years of age, and can mentally tune into different images of God at will. God is always smiling and optimistic. Sometimes God is busy and can't be seen anywhere, but God's members take great delight in making contact with me instead, waving and shouting and smiling down at me. I can only cope with a few seconds of contact with God, and fleeting images of all God's members, because of the enormous amount of activity in Heaven. A typical visit to God goes something like this:

> I look deeply into the back of my mind, and sometimes it helps to cast my eyes towards the sky. One of God's faces eventually comes into view. I say "How are you, God?". "I'm great, busy as a bee", replies God. "Thanks for a wonderful day, God". "My pleasure", comes a happy sounding voice. Then God disappears into the brightness and I feel happy, and I resume my usual activities.

Sometimes God's face is so enormous that I think that I must be looking at a giant, almost as big as the earth's diameter. Other times, there are visions of ordinary looking men and women of different nationalities and persuasions.

I know that God is the greatest friend that I will ever have, although I am also aware that my contribution to the friendship is not ideal. God once told me that it would make Her/Him very happy if I tried my best to make the earth a happy place, with lots of smiling and laughing and feelings of goodwill. I never ask God for anything, since I know that God is responsible for all the major events in my life. God told me that She/He didn't want any payment or reward for help, although a word of thanks is always appreciated.

Sometimes when my life isn't going smoothly, I am tempted to visit God to ask for help, but at the last second I refrain, knowing that such a gesture would be ungrateful and might sadden God. For example, once I desperately wanted a job with a large prestigious firm of solicitors, and contemplated asking God to intercede on my behalf. Luckily I didn't go begging to my best friend, since I got the job soon afterwards anyway. This type of thing happens to me frequently, and although I am initially disappointed, in the long run events turn out for the best.

Many people take their best friend for granted, but I am convinced that a simple "Thank you" is the least I can do.

So all my encounters with God are very simple and brief:

> "Hi God, I just called to say thanks.
> Mind yourself. Bye"

Sometimes these encounters are fast and furious, done on the spur of the moment, invariably making God burst out laughing, and She/He asks "What's all the hurry for?", or if She/He is busy, a wink and a smile would be my reply.

☐

Before I became friends with God, I had a conventional religious upbringing, attending church every week, and participating in all the usual ceremonies. Adolescence, of course, brought big physical and mental changes, especially a rebellion against my religion. My parents were equally stubborn, and couldn't for a long time accept this turn of events. Many hours were spent hotly and loudly arguing over the pros and cons of church-going.

This rebellion against religion was extremely difficult and heart rending for me, for I am good at heart, although I have an independent spirit, and it lasted for a couple of years. In my childhood years, church-going was an integral part of my life, and I loved the pageantry of the various ceremonies. Retreats, sodalities, processions, all had great appeal. I loved the smell of incense, and the singing of hymns in both Latin and English. Church was also a great social occasion, when I met and saw all the neighbours, and as a young teenager, I loved to see and be seen by the local boys. In my mid-teens, I developed a great interest in church architecture and organ music. But in all those years, I never once saw or met God.

I was heart-broken at the thought of leaving the church, and all its lovely activities and symbols, but also very bitter at the absurdity of it all. It always struck me as daft that I never actually enrolled in the church of my own will, and so I started looking around for some other church I might like to join, but to no avail. Gradually the pain of leaving my church eased, and slowly I gained confidence in myself and my mental and spiritual freedom. Throughout these few years, I had no-one who agreed with my views, making the task even more lonely and testing.

During this period, I always acknowledged the existance of a God, but in a logical or scientific sort of way.

I emerged from this long experience as a stronger and more independent-minded person, and was better able to focus on my future life and career.

As the years went by, I did well in life, both academically and socially. Every so often, I felt grateful to be alive and so happy, until one day I realised that I couldn't take all the credit for my good life, and God must be smiling on me. I was amazed at how simple it was to contact God, and we got on like a "house on fire" from day One. We have been friends ever since.

☐

My husband, Sam, is a kindred spirit, and went through the same "Rites of Passage" to make friends with God as I did. No doubt our mutual friend God arranged for us to meet and marry. Thanks to God also, we have two lovely children.

The years rolled by, and as our children blossomed before our eyes, we were constantly reminded of our own childhood. Every day, some little event or word would rekindle a far away memory and give us a better appreciation of our own development. All the local schools adhered to one or another religious philosophy, so we accepted religious knowledge as another school subject to be learned by our children. Sam and I have learned to accept that other people are free to follow any religion they choose, but we expect tolerance of our own non-belief in return. Both our children are now in their twenties, and they are still Christians.

Sam and I have always known that millions of people derive great happiness and comfort from adherence to their chosen or family religion, and in many cases, church attendance is the only social event of the week or month, so has both spiritual and psychological benefits.

Over the years, Sam and I have attended many funerals, weddings, and baptisms, with our friends and relations, accompanied by all the feelings of happiness and sadness appropriate to the event. These occasions are an integral part of life, and have to be celebrated and acknowledged as milestones. But besides having a few drinks or a meal, what meaningful public gesture can be made to God by people who don't subscribe to conventional religious philosophies? Of course, in private, hours can be spent thanking God. Nevertheless, people are social creatures, and want to show their happiness in public. Sam and I came up with a wonderful idea, which I will share with you in the following chapters.

CHAPTER 2

In those early years, I was like a "golf widow", except that Sam's excuse was not golf. He had spent about 12 months scouring the city for a suitable building to use as an Appreciation Centre. Then one March, he struck gold, when he found an old house in its own grounds, which had a big hall and staircase, with a big stained glass dome overhead.

Luckily, the Building Societies and Banks were flush with money, and weren't over cautious about advancing us a mortgage to buy this lovely old house. Some of the neighbours weren't too pleased to see our Planning Application in the name of "Friends of God", presuming us to be another fringe religion. After the residents association's appeal to the Planning Board, we eventually obtained our Planning Permission with a string of conditions attached. Next delay was in getting our Fire Safety Certificate, but eventually the builder started on site.

We removed the entire staircase to create a two-storey hall. The stained glass was removed from the dome and stored away, with the intention of providing a colourful dome over a smaller room at a later date, as funds permitted. Then the inside of the dome was plastered and painted black, while the outside was covered with a waterproofing membrane. I choose a maroon colour for the paint on the walls, and a cream coloured wool carpet, complimented by fawn and yellow armchairs in a circle around the perimeter of the hall. We had no interest in pictures or other ornaments for this special hall.

Sam spent a long time organising the production of a video, since most people thought he was mad, but eventually money spoke louder than sentiment.

A hi-fi system was next on the agenda, capable of recording onto cassettes.

I love gardening, so in the meantime, I was busy rejuvenating the front and rear gardens, now in full bloom.

During all this mad burst of building activity, my sister Rose was also "blooming", while expecting her first child, and co-incidentally, a beautiful boy was born a week before our project was finished. Keith was duly baptised in my sister's church, but she and her husband Don sceptically accepted my invitation to a Thanksgiving in our new Appreciation Centre.

□

I'll never forget that first Saturday morning. God was smiling on us, because the sun was beaming down, making the flowers and lawns look beautiful. Sam and I put on our best clothes. There were about fifteen people including family and friends, not forgetting Keith, who occasionally let a yell to remind everyone that he was boss.

We were glad to seek coolness inside our Centre, and everyone relaxed in a circle in the armchairs. We put Rose, Don, and Keith on a white leatherette two-seater sofa in the centre, and Sam dimmed the lights. The projector beamed a galaxy of stars and planets onto the black dome, accompanied by Clarke's "Trumpet Voluntary" on the CD player. Gradually, images of famous people throughout history, intermingled with the stars and each other, until eventually the dome was a kaleidoscope of colour and shape and mystery and magic. The music was lowered, and Sam's tape-recorded voice emanated from the loud-speakers:

"Hello God, how are you"

"I'm delighted to see all my friends and a new baby friend", replied God.

"I imagine you must be up to your eyes at the moment, God, but I won't delay you for long. My sister-in-law, Rose, and her husband Don, are absolutely thrilled with their first baby, Keith, and have asked me to say a very big Thank You".

"I know, Sam, because Rose couldn't find enough words of happiness and gratitude, the very second she saw Keith for the first time, and heard his first healthy cry".

"Well, that's all, God, and we really mean Thanks. Goodbye".

"All the best, and see you soon, my friends".

With that, there was silence and darkness as the video and hi-fi were switched off. Then there was a big clap and applause from everyone, and as the lights slowly came back on, Rose was seen to be crying happily and her baby fast asleep (or at least as quiet as a mouse).

We sat around for an hour or two, everyone talking excitedly, and enjoyed sandwiches and snacks, washed down by tea and coffee or soft drinks. Some of us enjoyed the sunshine and flowers in the garden.

One by one, the party broke up, and as Rose, Don, and Keith prepared to depart, I gave them a little memento of our meeting, a brass plaque with all the details – date, time, weight, hospital, midwife, doctor, parents, address, etc – and a tape recording of the party.

☐

This was the first of many such happy Birth Thanksgivings, and a variety of themes evolved. Sam and I took turns at answering as God, and some parents participated in the conversation. Occasionally there was only one parent present. Sam and I spent time with the family beforehand, to discuss the form of the conversation, and more often than not, they choose their own words, which they imagined would be spoken by God in the circumstances. We also had five standard conversations, some jolly and friendly, others more reserved and serious. All of the conversations were pre-recorded, but a few people opted for a live session. Now and again, parents just said a few words of thanks to God, without any music or videos. At the end of the day, most people just wanted to put on record that they were extremely grateful to their God for a wonderful gift.

CHAPTER 3

A few weeks later, we held our second Thanksgiving, the marriage of a friend's daughter, and I was very excited at the prospect, hoping for a glittering occasion, with lots of silk and lace. The girl came from the city, and her husband hailed from South Africa, hoping to graduate as a doctor in the next year. The happy couple arrived on a Wednesday evening, shortly after the last signing in the Registry Office, attired in their Sunday Best, but no expensive designer creations. Only her parents and a few friends from both sides were present, although more flamboyantly dressed than the wedded couple.

The day was pleasant with not too much sunshine, so we were able to relax outdoors for about ten minutes before going inside. Ahmed and Violet had given me their favourite CD – Sanson Ki Mala Peh Simroon Bhajan, by Nusrat Fateh Ali Khan, which I thought was a good choice of music. A few days previously, Ahmed had given me photos of famous people from the world of Islam, which Sam managed to incorporate into the video. Violet had drawn a sketch of a face which she thought was very God-like, and which fitted in very well with the other video images.

When the lights went down, the music and video seemed very appropriate.

"Hope its not too late to call you, God".

"You're as welcome as the flowers in May, I never sleep" replied God.

"Two lovely people from different parts of your Earth have asked me to make contact with you. Ahmed and Violet know that out of millions of people in the world, it was no coincidence that they met and fell in love. They strongly suspect that you were "pulling strings".

"I have my ways and means" laughed God, "but Ahmed and Violet did most of the talking together, and made a big effort to overcome the differences in their respective upbringings".

"They are naturally slightly apprehensive about their future together, God, but know that you will help them over any hurdles along the road".

"Once I see them doing their best, I will do the rest".

"Violet and Ahmed are especially happy now, God, and want to say Thank You for bringing them together, and giving them such fulfilment".

"No need to thank me, they largely have themselves to thank, although I'm chuffed at the compliment".

"Well, goodbye, God, and thanks a million".

"All the best, Violet and Ahmed, and by the way, I love your choice of music for the occasion".

After a brief pause, a nice piece of classical music was played at a low volume, and then the lights were slowly switched on. Big smiles all around, and lots of hand shaking and embraces, brought the Thanksgiving to a happy conclusion.

No wedding is complete without lots of photos, despite the fact that the sun had set. No one was in any hurry to leave, so a light supper was served. We presented everyone with a plaque and tape in remembrance of the Thanksgiving.

Violet's parents were very pleased with the occasion, despite having been deprived of a conventional church wedding. Violet and Ahmed have been back for other Thanksgivings over the years, for themselves and as guests of friends, and I can vouch that God kept Her/His promise and they kept theirs to each other.

CHAPTER 4

Sam had great difficulty in devising a suitable ceremony for a Death Thanksgiving, which normally tends to be a sad occasion. Non-religious tend to go for cremations instead of burials, although both options are applicable.

We decided that, in fact, Death was probably the most appropriate time to thank God, more important than birth or marriage or other big occasions. Mourners are sad at the loss of a relative or friend, for hundreds of reasons, but God had a hand in all of those reasons, and so deserves the ultimate Thank You. You often hear people say "Wasn't it wonderful she had no pain when she died, or only a short illness". Even if your child dies in a car accident, weren't you fortunate to have a few years bliss, whereas someone else might have no children. In short, God creates and manages life, and without our friends and relations, our lives would be barren.

So at our Thanksgivings, we seek and dwell on all the positive aspects of life and death. Some people mourn because they feel sorry for themselves, possibly having neglected the deceased in recent years. But Thanks to God is still worthwhile, for your early association with the deceased.

Our first Death Thanksgiving was nerve wracking. Bill was 81 when he died of cancer in hospital. His wife,

Deirdre, who was 65, was heart-broken, because they had enjoyed a really good marriage. It was their daughter, Laura, who made all the funeral arrangements. Bill and Deirdre were non-religious, but Laura had joined a Protestant Church when she was about twenty-five. Both Laura's parents loved music, so trying to decide on Bill's favourite piece was very difficult, but in the end, she and Deirdre choose a song that most reminded them of Bill, "To the Unknown Man" by Vangelis.

The coffin bearing Bill's body was brought straight from the hospital mortuary to the cemetery crematorium, where a Protestant clergyman said a few nice words, and then Bill's coffin disappeared amidst many sorrowful tears. Laura told me that there was a large attendance at the cemetery, and it seems that about half of these decided to continue on to our Appreciation Centre. When an avalanche of cars arrived, we didn't know what hit us. Cars parked on the lawn, and clogged up the public pavement. Sam was forced to remove all the furniture from the centre, except a central settee for Deirdre and Laura to sit on. I don't know how everyone crammed in, but many tummy muscles must have been exercised. Some people were surprised to hear the music, no doubt expecting sad and lonesome sounds. One or two people sobbed quietly.

"Hello everyone" hailed a voice from nowhere, "why all the sad faces? Bill did me proud on Earth, never once let me down. Do you remember, Deirdre, when Bill carried you across that mucky lane, and then proposed to you in the field with cows all around you? And Laura, that time when you were sleepwalking, and Bill pulled you out of the swimming pool? And Brian, when Bill tipped you off about the impending liquidation of your biggest supplier? Or do you remember, Jane, when you were very lonely and depressed in your bedsitter, and Bill's kind voice pulled you through?"

"But why couldn't you have left him here with us for a few more years, God" Laura asked.

"Bill was suffering tremendous pain, Laura, physical and mental, because he couldn't bear just lying in bed so helpless, month in, month out. I gave you all plenty of Bill's time during a long life, and now he is of great help to me in a project, and as happy as ever he was".

"Well, God", Deirdre said, "you gave me the best present anyone could wish for when you gave me Bill, and I am so proud that he is still so good that you want him back. I cannot thank you enough for that opportunity".

"Thanks, God, for giving me such a wonderful father and friend", Laura said.

Just then a man in the Centre shouted out:

"Tell Bill that he lost his bet when he always boasted that he would outlive me".

That was the voice of Bill's best friend, Fred, and caused a slight ripple of laughter.

Everyone seemed to have cheered up, so God said:

"Thanks for contacting me, and don't be too long before the next visit".

Various people said afterwards that they thought that they saw God on the domed ceiling, and naturally their descriptions of Her/Him varied according to their mood and life experiences.

The assembled crowd ate us out completely that day, but Sam and I agreed hours later when everyone was gone, that the occasion was a great send-off for Bill, and a proud moment for Deirdre and Laura. We got a lot of stick from the neighbours because of all the cars and noise, so we had to make different arrangements for the next Death Thanksgiving, which included bus transport to and from the cemetery, and opening up the smaller rooms to accommodate the overflow of people. Occasionally we can't cope with big crowds, but there are now a few larger Appreciation Centres in the city, which we hire out for the day.

CHAPTER 5

Sometimes we hold Collective Thanksgivings, which can be complicated for Sam to organise. Usually about twenty to thirty people give Thanks to God for any number of reasons, generally everyday things which affect their particular lives. One particular Autumn day sticks out in my memory and went something like this:

> "Top of the morning, God. Some friends of yours would like a word".

> "Well, you've really got a mixed gathering today, Sam, some of whom haven't made contact with me for years, and one or two who really give me a hard time. I am looking forward to this".

> "Mary Louise wants to Thank You for sparing her farm from the terrible flood last winter, which resulted in neighbour's fields being submerged, but not hers". This was accompanied by Tchaikovsky's "Swan Lake".

> "Martin can't believe he came through the triple by-pass heart operation". Accompanied by Louis Armstrong "What a Wonderful World".

"God, you're some task master. You let me slog it out for twelve rounds in the boxing ring, to win by one point, but making me realise that it was high time to retire". Accompanied by John Mayall "Broken Wings".

"I thought I was a gonner last week when I skidded on the road into the path of that oncoming articulated truck. I got a funny feeling afterwards that you had stage-managed the whole thing, to shock me into improving my driving". Accompanied by "Walking in the Sunshine" by Roger Miller.

"That mad Alsatian dog nearly had me for dinner that time, but I sometimes wonder why the dog and the motor-cycle rider had to die in the crash". Accompanied by Beethoven's "Moonlight Sonata".

"My mother wouldn't let me marry that man from Valencia, which almost drove me to suicide, but luckily at the last moment, I saw him with my own eyes, wheeling the pram in Madrid. Will I ever find the right man?"

Accompanied by Puccini "O Mio Babbino Caro".

"I love my new house. If I had waited a few more months, I couldn't afford to buy it because of the huge rise in prices in the meantime". Accompanied by Chopin's "Minute Waltz".

"When I drove off with the handbrake still on during my driving test, my heart sank. You must have sent that pretty girl sauntering along the street, just to distract my examiner, because he passed me first time". Accompanied by "Elsewhere" by Vangelis.

"Thanks a million (three million in fact) for winning the Lottery, but I don't want the money, so maybe you will guide me in doing some good work in the Third World?" Accompanied by "Money" by The Who.

At this point, everyone seemed to go mad and rushed to Tom with wild suggestions and advice on how to spend his money. But they stopped dead in their tracks, when the last piece of music, on the organ, Toccata and Fugue in E Minor, burst into life. Two minutes later, a little girl with her mother said:

> "Thanks, God, for getting me this lovely motorised wheelchair". Accompanied by Howard Blake's "Walking in the Air".

I could see God looking on in great amusement at all this.

> "I'm speechless" God said. "Thanks a bunch for this great show. Don't thank me, thank yourselves. Bye for now and keep in touch".

Chapter 6

After the first Birth Thanksgiving, we advertised in one or two newspapers, letting everyone know that they could give Thanks to God for anything, and it made no difference if they were religious or not, or what colour or race they were. Most of the people who come are non-religious, and enjoy the informality and relaxed atmosphere, since there are no rules about formal dress or otherwise. Quite a number of people come immediatly after a more formal wedding ceremony in a church or Registry Office, and naturally there is a lot of style and excitement on these occasions. Our garden has become very popular for photographs.

In general, Thanksgivings are held for Births, Marriages, and Deaths, but any excuse is justified. People come after passing the driving test, after passing exams, after getting a new job or promotion, after buying a house, or recovering from illness or an accident, and upon retirement, etc.

Sam and I have only one Golden Rule - no one could ask God for anything (except obviously in the privacy of their own lives). You could not even ask God for forgiveness for a misdemeanour - in such cases, you had to believe that She/He had already forgiven you, and therefore, you simply had to say sorry, and Thank God for Her/His gift.

Year by year, we improved our Appreciation Centre, and we converted a few of the other rooms into more private Centres. A large number of people come as individuals to give thanks, or in couples, or sometimes just a small group of four or five. The main emphasis is on peace, quiet, and privacy. The general public is never admitted, although they sometimes try to "gate-crash".

Over the years, many people brought their own individual style to different occasions. Most people have favourite pieces of music, and we regularly play their own CD's and cassettes and LP's. Once or twice, we were given videos to play, although these tended to be a bit amateurish.

We operate our Appreciation Centre along business lines, since the Building Society mortgage has to be paid, and we need a salary to live on. We have a set of standard charges for the different Thanksgivings. Thanks to God, we make a good livelihood. There was great potential for expansion and building new Centres in different cities, but we opted to provide a top-class service in our single Centre.

Many people have copied us since, some introducing innovative ideas, others providing more large and plush surroundings, and in general, the standards are very professional, and improving day by day. Occasionally, a "bad apple" arrives on the scene, but market forces eventually drive him out.

One little idea that we have tried to foster over the years, is a suggestion to our clients to make a donation to the charity of their choice, preferably soon after the Thanksgiving, but we don't act as agents for any charities. "If only my daughter would get better, I would pay anything to the doctor" is a frequently heard phrase. So if a healthy child is born, don't forget to keep even a part of your promise. Thanks to God sounds more meaningful when it is accompanied by a little sacrifice, and God would prefer this gesture to go towards making Earth a happier planet.

END

www.ingramcontent.com/pod-product-compliance
Lightning Source LLC
Chambersburg PA
CBHW060604030426
42337CB00019B/3604